"Revolutionizing Reality:

The Apple Vision Pro Unveiled"

TABLE OF CONTENTS

Introduction

"Revolutionizing Realities with Apple Vision Pro"

In the ever-evolving landscape of technology, one groundbreaking innovation has captured the imagination of users and industry enthusiasts alike—the Apple Vision Pro. As we embark on a journey through the realms of spatial computing, this book explores the transformative impact of Apple's latest foray into the world of Virtual Reality (VR). Beyond the buzzwords and technical specifications, we will unravel the significance of Apple's entry into VR and provide an insightful overview of the mesmerizing Apple Vision Pro

A. Navigating the VR Landscape

Virtual Reality, once a futuristic concept, has now become a tangible reality, immersing users in a digital realm that transcends traditional boundaries. The VR landscape has witnessed rapid evolution, from early experiments to sophisticated, immersive experiences across diverse industries. Gaming, education, healthcare, and entertainment have all felt the transformative touch of VR, creating a demand for innovative solutions that blend seamlessly with our daily lives.

B. Apple's Ascent into Virtual Realms

Amidst the myriad players in the VR arena, Apple's entry brings a distinctive blend of innovation, design prowess, and a commitment to user-centric technology. The significance of Apple's venture into VR extends beyond the mere introduction of a new device. It signifies a strategic move by a tech giant to redefine the standards of spatial computing. Apple's unique approach, characterized by an unwavering focus on simplicity and user experience, is poised to leave an indelible mark on the VR landscape.

C. Unveiling the Apple Vision Pro

At the heart of this exploration is the Apple Vision Pro, a spatial computer designed to seamlessly meld the digital and physical realms. This revolutionary device promises to reshape the way we work, communicate, and experience entertainment. As pre-orders open and the release date approaches, anticipation builds for a device that could redefine the very fabric of our digital interactions.

VisionOS, a bespoke operating system rooted in Apple's decades-long engineering heritage, powers the

Apple Vision Pro. The interface is not merely an evolution but a revolution, responding to the user's eyes, hands, and voice. In the words of Tim Cook, Apple's CEO, "The era of spatial computing has arrived," and the Apple Vision Pro is positioned as the pinnacle of this evolution—a device that transcends the boundaries of conventional consumer electronics.

As we embark on this exploration of the Apple Vision Pro, the subsequent chapters will delve into its features, design philosophy, and the potential impact on diverse aspects of our lives. Join us in unraveling the magic and innovation that define Apple's latest venture into the realm of spatial computing.

PART I

The Arrival of Spatial Computing:

Shaping the Future with Apple Vision Pro

In the ever-evolving landscape of technology, the arrival of spatial computing marks a pivotal moment, ushering in a new era of interaction and immersion. This chapter delves into the definition and importance of spatial computing, introduces the innovative visionOS powering the Apple Vision Pro, and explores Tim Cook's visionary statement on the profound impact of spatial computing in our digital lives.

A. Definition and Importance of Spatial Computing

Spatial computing represents a paradigm shift in the way we engage with digital content, breaking free from the constraints of traditional interfaces. At its core, spatial computing involves the seamless integration of the digital world into our physical reality, creating an immersive and interactive experience. It leverages technologies such as augmented reality (AR) and virtual reality (VR) to merge digital elements with the real world, transforming how we perceive and interact with information.

The importance of spatial computing lies in its ability to enhance user experiences across various domains. By bridging the gap between the physical and digital realms, spatial computing opens avenues for more intuitive interactions. From gaming and entertainment to productivity and collaboration, the applications of spatial computing are vast and varied.

The Apple Vision Pro, with its focus on spatial computing, promises to redefine these interactions, offering users a revolutionary way to work, connect, and explore.

B. Introduction to visionOS and Its Foundation in macOS, iOS, and iPadOS

Central to the transformative capabilities of the Apple Vision Pro is the innovative operating system, visionOS. This bespoke system represents the culmination of decades of engineering innovation rooted in

Apple's macOS, iOS, and iPadOS ecosystems. Unlike traditional operating systems, visionOS is tailored specifically for spatial computing, providing a three-dimensional user interface and input system that respond to the user's eyes, hands, and voice.

The integration of visionOS across Apple's diverse product line ensures a seamless ecosystem where users can transition effortlessly between devices. This cross-platform compatibility enhances the overall user experience, allowing individuals to harness the power of spatial computing not only on the Apple

Vision Pro but also on Macs, iPhones, and iPads. This interconnectedness aligns with Apple's overarching philosophy of creating a cohesive and user-centric ecosystem that adapts to the needs and preferences of its users.

C. Tim Cook's Statement on the Era of Spatial Computing

At the helm of Apple's vision for the future is Tim Cook, the CEO whose leadership has seen the company evolve and innovate across multiple dimensions. Cook's visionary statement on the era of spatial computing serves as a compass guiding Apple towards uncharted territories. In his words, "The era of spatial computing has arrived," Cook encapsulates the profound impact and transformative potential of spatial computing on how we interact with technology.

Cook's statement reflects a broader perspective on the evolution of computing paradigms. Spatial computing, as envisioned by Apple, transcends traditional interfaces, unlocking new possibilities for work, communication, and entertainment. By acknowledging the arrival of this era, Cook signals Apple's commitment to being at the forefront of this technological revolution. The

Apple Vision Pro becomes a tangible embodiment of this commitment, a device designed not merely to keep pace with technological advancements but to set new standards and redefine user expectations.

As we delve deeper into the chapters that follow, the focus will shift to the practical manifestations of spatial computing within the Apple Vision Pro. The promises of seamless navigation, intuitive interactions, and immersive experiences will be explored, providing readers with a comprehensive understanding of the transformative power of spatial computing and its embodiment in Apple's latest innovation. Join us on this journey as we navigate the uncharted territories of spatial computing with the Apple Vision Pro at the helm.

PART II. Unveiling Apple Vision Pro: A Glimpse into the Future of Spatial Computing

The curtains rise, and the spotlight falls upon Apple's latest masterpiece—the Apple Vision Pro. This chapter takes you on a journey through the unveiling of this groundbreaking spatial computer, exploring release information, delving into Tim Cook's visionary perspective, and dissecting the key features and capabilities that make the Apple Vision Pro a herald of the future.

A. Release Information and Availability

As anticipation reached a crescendo, Apple officially announced the arrival of the Apple Vision Pro, setting the stage for a new era in spatial computing. The device is scheduled to grace U.S. Apple Store locations and the online store starting February 2, marking a momentous occasion for tech enthusiasts and Apple aficionados alike. However, the journey begins even earlier, with pre-orders slated to commence on January 19 at 5 a.m. PST.

The decision to make the Apple Vision Pro available both in-store and online underscores Apple's commitment to accessibility. By providing customers with multiple avenues to obtain their coveted spatial computer, Apple ensures a broad reach, allowing users to seamlessly integrate this revolutionary device into their lives.

The release information not only marks a date on the calendar but symbolizes a technological milestone—a moment when the world gets its hands on a device that promises to reshape digital interactions and transcend the boundaries of conventional consumer electronics.

B. Tim Cook's Vision for Apple Vision Pro

At the heart of every groundbreaking Apple product is a vision—Tim Cook's vision for a future where technology seamlessly integrates into the fabric of everyday life. As the CEO of Apple, Cook is not merely a leader; he is a visionary steering the company towards uncharted territories. His perspective on the Apple Vision Pro is nothing short of transformative.

In Cook's own words, "The era of spatial computing has arrived." This succinct statement encapsulates the essence of Apple's venture into VR and spatial computing. It signifies not just the introduction of a new device but a paradigm shift—an acknowledgment that our interaction with technology is entering a new dimension. Cook's vision positions the Apple Vision Pro as a harbinger of change, heralding an era where the digital and physical worlds coalesce seamlessly.

Cook's leadership has consistently emphasized user-centric design, simplicity, and innovation. His vision for the Apple Vision Pro extends beyond the confines of a product launch; it articulates a broader philosophy—an unwavering commitment to pushing the boundaries of what technology can achieve. As readers, we are invited to explore this vision, to understand how spatial computing, as envisaged by Tim Cook, has the potential to redefine our relationship with technology.

C. Key Features and Capabilities

The Apple Vision Pro isn't just a device; it's a convergence of cutting-edge technology, meticulous design, and user-centric innovation.

Let's unravel the key features and capabilities that set this spatial computer apart, promising a revolution in how we work, connect, and explore.

i. VisionOS: A Three-Dimensional User Interface

At the core of the Apple Vision Pro experience is VisionOS, a bespoke operating system that draws upon the rich heritage of macOS, iOS, and iPadOS. VisionOS introduces a three-dimensional user interface, responding to the user's eyes, hands, and voice. This isn't a mere evolution of existing operating systems; it's a revolution in how we navigate and interact with digital content.

ii. Intuitive Gestures for Seamless Navigation

The era of buttons and touchscreens takes a backseat as intuitive gestures come to the forefront. Users can interact with apps simply by looking at them, tapping fingers to select, flicking wrists to scroll, or using a virtual keyboard or dictation to type. This marks a departure from conventional input methods, ushering in an era where the user's natural movements become the language of interaction.

iii. Immersive Environments for Expanded Experiences

With Environments, the Apple Vision Pro invites users to step beyond the physical confines of a room. Dynamic landscapes like Haleakalā, Joshua Tree, and Yosemite national parks, or even the surface of the moon, become immersive backdrops. The Digital

Crown, a novel input method, empowers users to control the level of immersion, providing a customizable and captivating experience.

iv. Unleashing the Power of 1 Million Apps

Compatibility is key, and the Apple Vision Pro boasts access to over 1 million compatible apps across iOS and iPadOS. These apps seamlessly integrate into the spatial computing environment, offering users a familiar yet enhanced experience. The all-new App Store for the Apple Vision Pro is a gateway to spatial computing experiences, setting the stage for a diverse and dynamic ecosystem.

v. Productivity Amplified: From Fantastical to Microsoft 365

The Apple Vision Pro isn't just a plaything; it's a productivity powerhouse. Key apps like Fantastical, Freeform, JigSpace, Microsoft 365, and Slack find a new canvas on the three-dimensional interface. Multitasking becomes a breeze, with apps appearing side by side at any scale, providing the ultimate workspace. Support for Magic Keyboard and Magic Trackpad enhances the user's ability to create the perfect digital workspace.

vi. The Ultimate Entertainment Experience

When it comes to entertainment, the Apple Vision Pro raises the bar. Ultra-high-resolution displays surpassing 4K TV quality immerse users in movies and TV shows from Apple TV+, Disney+, Max, and other services. The Apple TV app offers access to more than 150 3D titles with incredible depth. Apple Immersive Video, a pioneering format, places users inside the action with 180-degree, three-dimensional 8K recordings captured with Spatial Audio. New gaming experiences, including titles like NBA 2K24 Arcade Edition and Sonic Dream Team, showcase the device's prowess in transforming the gaming landscape.

vii. Memories Brought to Life

The Apple Vision Pro isn't just about the present; it's a vessel for reliving memories in entirely new ways. Spatial photos and videos transport users back to special moments, enhanced by Spatial Audio for an immersive experience. The device seamlessly integrates with the iPhone 15 Pro and iPhone 15 Pro Max, allowing users to capture spatial videos on the go and relive them on the Apple Vision Pro. It's not just a screen; it's a portal to memories that come alive.

viii. FaceTime Becomes Spatial Communication takes a leap into the future with FaceTime on the Apple Vision Pro. Life-size appearances on video calls, Spatial Audio for realistic voice locations, and the introduction of Persona—a spatial representation that captures facial expressions and hand movements in real time. Whether in a personal or professional setting, FaceTime on the Apple Vision Pro transcends the limitations of conventional video calls.

ix. Breakthrough Design for Personalization

The Apple Vision Pro is not just a marvel of technology; it's a design masterpiece. A modular system allows users to personalize their fit, ensuring both comfort and functionality. A singular piece of three-dimensionally formed, laminated glass flows into a custom aluminum alloy frame, encapsulating an astonishing amount of technology in a compact design. The Light Seal, made of soft textile, and flexible straps ensure a precise fit, while ZEISS Optical Inserts cater to users with vision correction needs.

x. Unrivaled Innovation with Apple Silicon

The powerhouse driving the Apple Vision Pro's unparalleled performance lies in its dual-chip design. The M2 chip delivers standalone performance, while the brand-new R1 chip processes input from 12 cameras, five sensors, and six microphones. This unique design, combined with micro-OLED technology packing 23 million pixels into two displays, sets the Apple Vision Pro apart as an unparalleled feat of innovation.

xi. Privacy and Security at the Core

In a world where privacy is paramount, the Apple Vision Pro sets the gold standard. Optic ID, a new authentication system, analyzes a user's iris for secure unlocking, password autofill, and Apple Pay transactions. Eye tracking information remains private during navigation, not shared with Apple or third-party apps. The groundbreaking EyeSight feature ensures transparency, making the device appear transparent when a user interacts with others, thus providing visual cues about the user's focus.

xii. Accessibility in visionOS

True to Apple's commitment to accessibility, visionOS incorporates powerful features tailored for spatial computing. From VoiceOver and Zoom to Switch Control and Guided Access, users can interact with the Apple Vision Pro entirely using their eyes, hands, or voice, catering to a diverse range of needs. VisionOS allows users to choose their preferred input method, ensuring an inclusive and personalized experience.

xiii. Environmentally Conscious Design
Beyond its technological marvels, the Apple Vision Pro embraces environmental responsibility.

Incorporating 100 percent recycled rare earth elements, tin soldering, and aluminum in its construction, the device adheres to Apple's high standards for sustainability. The packaging, too, reflects a commitment to reducing plastics, aligning with Apple's broader goal of eliminating plastics in all packaging by 2025. This conscious design extends to the device's energy efficiency, meeting Apple's carbon-neutral goals for global operations.

Conclusion: A Glimpse into Tomorrow

As we conclude our journey through the unveiling of the Apple Vision Pro, the significance of this spatial computer becomes abundantly clear. It is not merely a device; it is a vessel transporting us into a future where spatial computing transforms the way we perceive and interact with our digital world.

The release information and availability mark the beginning of a new chapter, where users can embrace the Apple Vision Pro and integrate its capabilities into their daily lives. Tim Cook's vision for this spatial computer extends beyond a product launch—it's a declaration that the era of spatial computing has indeed arrived, and Apple is at the forefront of this technological revolution.

The key features and capabilities unravel a device that goes beyond the expected, pushing the boundaries of what is possible. From the immersive three-dimensional interface of VisionOS to the privacy-centric design, from the entertainment prowess to the environmentally conscious construction, the Apple Vision Pro stands as a testament to innovation, user-centric design, and a commitment to a sustainable future.

As we step into this new era of spatial computing with the Apple Vision Pro, the chapters that follow will delve deeper into specific aspects, providing a comprehensive understanding of how this device will impact various facets of our lives. Join us on this exploration as we unravel the layers of innovation, technology, and user experience that define the Apple Vision Pro—a glimpse into tomorrow, available today.

PART III. visionOS: A Revolutionary Operating System

In the heart of the Apple Vision Pro lies a transformative force — visionOS, an operating system that redefines the user experience. This chapter delves into the revolutionary features of visionOS, exploring its three-dimensional user interface, the seamless integration of intuitive gestures and controls using eyes, hands, and voice, and the captivating world of Immersive Environments coupled with the innovative Digital Crown.

A. Three-Dimensional User Interface

At the core of visionOS is a paradigm-shifting three-dimensional user interface, representing a departure from traditional operating systems. Drawing upon decades of engineering innovation in macOS, iOS, and iPadOS, visionOS creates a spatial computing environment that responds to the user's every glance, touch, and spoken command.

The three-dimensional interface is not just a visual spectacle; it's a functional evolution. Users can navigate through a world that extends beyond the flat screens of traditional devices. Apps, previously confined to two-dimensional displays, now exist in a three-dimensional space, offering a more immersive and intuitive interaction. This breakthrough introduces a new dimension to computing, where the digital and physical realms seamlessly intertwine.

One of the hallmarks of the three-dimensional user interface is its ability to adapt to the user's perspective. As users move, the interface dynamically adjusts, creating a sense of continuity and fluidity. This adaptability enhances the overall user experience, ensuring that the spatial environment feels like an extension of the user's natural movements and interactions.

B. Intuitive Gestures and Controls Using Eyes, Hands, and Voice

The era of buttons and touchscreens takes a backseat as visionOS introduces a new language of interaction — intuitive gestures and controls. Users can now navigate the Apple Vision Pro effortlessly using their eyes, hands, and voice, marking a significant departure from conventional input methods.

i. Eyes: The Window to Intuitive Interaction

The integration of eye tracking technology allows users to control the Apple Vision Pro by simply looking at elements on the screen. This groundbreaking feature not only enhances accessibility but also introduces a level of precision and responsiveness previously unseen in consumer electronics. The user's gaze becomes a powerful tool, enabling seamless navigation and interaction with apps, menus, and immersive environments.

ii. Hands: A Touch-Free Interface

Traditional touchscreens give way to a touch-free interface where users can interact with the Apple Vision Pro through hand gestures. Tapping fingers to select, flicking wrists to scroll, and even employing virtual keyboards or dictation for typing redefine how users engage with their digital environment. This shift from tactile to touch-free interaction enhances the overall accessibility and usability of the device.

iii. Voice: A Conversational Companion

Voice commands take center stage with visionOS, allowing users to control and navigate the Apple Vision Pro using natural language. Siri, Apple's intelligent virtual assistant, becomes a conversational companion, responding to voice commands to open or close apps, play media, and perform a myriad of tasks. This integration of voice as a primary input method aligns with the broader trend of making technology more accessible and user-friendly.

The combination of eye, hand, and voice controls creates a holistic and intuitive interaction model. Users can seamlessly transition between these input methods based on their preferences and the context of use, providing a versatile and personalized computing experience.

C. Immersive Environments and the Digital Crown

i. Immersive Environments: Extending Beyond Physical Boundaries

One of the defining features of visionOS is the concept of Immersive

Environments, transporting users beyond the physical constraints of their immediate surroundings. Dynamic and captivating landscapes like Haleakalā, Joshua Tree, and Yosemite national parks, or even the serene surface of the moon, serve as backdrops that users can immerse themselves in.

These environments are not mere visual adornments; they serve a practical purpose. In busy spaces, users can escape distractions by entering an environment that helps them focus. Conversely, in confined or monotonous settings, Immersive Environments offer a means to reduce clutter and introduce a refreshing change of scenery. This flexibility empowers users to customize their digital surroundings, creating a spatial experience that adapts to their needs and preferences.

ii. The Digital Crown: Empowering User Control

An innovative addition to the Apple Vision Pro is the Digital Crown, a versatile input method that empowers users to control the level of immersion in their chosen environment. By twisting the Digital Crown, users can adjust how present or immersed they are in an environment. This physical input method adds a tactile dimension to the user experience, allowing for precise control over the spatial elements.

The Digital Crown isn't merely a tool for adjusting immersion levels; it serves as a multifunctional interface element. Users can employ the Digital Crown to navigate through menus, zoom in or out, and perform other contextual actions. This dual functionality highlights Apple's commitment to providing users with a diverse and comprehensive set of controls, ensuring that the Apple

Vision Pro caters to a wide range of preferences and interaction styles.

Conclusion: Redefining Interaction in the Spatial Realm

In the tapestry of spatial computing, visionOS emerges as a thread that weaves together the fabric of the Apple Vision Pro's user experience. The three-dimensional user interface, intuitive gestures and controls, Immersive Environments, and the Digital Crown collectively redefine how users interact with digital content.

As we navigate the chapters ahead, the exploration will deepen, delving into specific applications and use cases that leverage the capabilities of visionOS. The Apple Vision Pro, guided by this revolutionary operating system, stands at the forefront of a new era in computing—one where the boundaries between the physical and digital worlds blur, and interaction becomes an immersive, intuitive, and personalized experience. Join us as we unravel the layers of innovation embedded in visionOS and witness the transformative impact it brings to the realm of spatial computing.

PART 4.

Extraordinary Experiences: Navigating the Three-Dimensional Frontier

In the landscape of spatial computing, Apple Vision Pro emerges as a torchbearer of extraordinary experiences, ushering users into a three-dimensional realm where multitasking, collaboration, and familiar apps undergo a transformative evolution. This chapter illuminates the exceptional facets of Apple Vision Pro, exploring the seamless integration of multitasking and collaboration in three-dimensional space, the infusion of familiar apps from iOS and iPadOS, and the immersive world of spatial computing experiences curated by the new App Store.

A. Multitasking and Collaboration in Three-Dimensional Space

The Apple Vision Pro transcends the conventional boundaries of multitasking, introducing a paradigm where users can collaborate and engage with apps in a three-dimensional space. This departure from the flat and restrictive nature of traditional displays fosters a workspace that is both expansive and dynamic.

i. Three-Dimensional Interface: A Canvas for Multitasking

The three-dimensional user interface of visionOS serves as the canvas for a new era of multitasking. Apps are no longer confined to a flat plane; they exist in the spatial realm, allowing users to arrange them side by side at any scale. This innovative approach provides an infinite canvas for productivity, enabling users to seamlessly switch between apps with intuitive gestures and controls.

Imagine editing a document while having a video call in a separate window, all within the same three-dimensional space. The Apple Vision Pro transforms multitasking into a fluid and natural experience, elevating productivity to unprecedented levels. Users can manipulate and interact with multiple apps simultaneously, breaking free from the constraints of traditional displays.

ii. Collaboration Redefined: A Shared Spatial Experience

Collaboration takes a giant leap forward as Apple Vision Pro invites users to share their spatial environment with others. Colleagues, friends, or family members can join the same three-dimensional space, creating a shared digital realm where collaboration becomes an immersive and engaging experience.

Whether it's co-editing documents, brainstorming ideas, or simply sharing a virtual space for a casual conversation, the collaborative possibilities are boundless. The spatial computing capabilities of Apple Vision Pro redefine the meaning of virtual collaboration, bringing a tangible and shared element to digital interactions.

B. Integration of Familiar Apps from iOS and iPadOS

The Apple Vision Pro seamlessly integrates familiar apps from the iOS and iPadOS ecosystems, expanding the device's capabilities and offering users a sense of continuity in their digital experiences. With over 1 million compatible apps, the transition to spatial computing becomes not just seamless but also enriching.

i. App Continuity: A Unified Digital Experience

Users familiar with iOS and iPadOS will find a sense of continuity as they explore the Apple Vision Pro. The transition from traditional devices to a spatial computing environment is facilitated by the presence of familiar apps that users have come to rely on. The three-dimensional interface serves as a natural evolution, allowing users to interact with their favorite apps in a more immersive and intuitive manner.

The integration of these apps extends beyond mere compatibility; they are optimized to leverage the spatial computing capabilities of Apple Vision Pro. Productivity apps like Fantastical, Freeform, and Microsoft 365 seamlessly adapt to the three-dimensional canvas, offering users a workspace that feels limitless. The learning curve is minimized, and users can effortlessly navigate the spatial environment, unlocking the full potential of these familiar tools.

ii. Magic Keyboard and Magic Trackpad: Enhancing the Experience

To complement the integration of familiar apps, Apple Vision Pro supports the use of the Magic

Keyboard and Magic Trackpad. This inclusion ensures that users can maintain a level of familiarity in their interactions while benefiting from the expanded capabilities of the three-dimensional interface.

The Magic Keyboard provides a tactile input method, catering to users who prefer the sensation of physical keys. The Magic Trackpad, on the other hand, offers a versatile and intuitive way to navigate the spatial environment, enhancing the overall user experience. This dual support for traditional input methods and spatial controls showcases Apple's commitment to providing users with options that suit their preferences.

C. Spatial Computing Experiences from the New App Store

The Apple Vision Pro introduces an all-new App Store tailored to the spatial computing landscape. With a curated selection of apps designed to harness the unique capabilities of Vision Pro, users can explore and download experiences that go beyond the ordinary. This section delves into the diverse and immersive world of spatial computing experiences available through the new App Store.

i. Apps Unleashed: A Gateway to Spatial Wonders

The App Store on Apple Vision Pro serves as a gateway to a treasure trove of spatial computing experiences. Developers have embraced the possibilities offered by the three-dimensional interface, creating apps that redefine entertainment, productivity, and creativity.

a. Productivity and Collaboration Apps

Apps like Freeform and JigSpace find new life on the Apple Vision Pro, offering users a spatial canvas for brainstorming, planning, and collaborating. The three-dimensional environment transforms the way teams work together, bringing a tangible and interactive element to virtual collaboration.

b. Entertainment and Gaming
The entertainment landscape undergoes a revolution with the Apple Vision Pro. Streaming services like Apple TV+, Disney+, and Max leverage ultra-high-resolution displays to immerse users in movies and TV shows. The introduction of Apple Immersive Video pioneers a new format, placing users inside the

action with three-dimensional, 8K recordings and Spatial Audio.

Gaming experiences reach new heights, with titles like NBA 2K24 Arcade Edition and Sonic Dream Team offering immersive gameplay on a screen as large as users desire. Spatial games, including Game Room, What the Golf?, and Super Fruit Ninja, leverage the powerful capabilities of Apple Vision Pro to transform the space around players, delivering unique and engaging experiences.

c. Spatial Photography and Video

The Apple Vision Pro elevates the art of capturing and reliving memories. Spatial photos and videos transport users back in time, providing an immersive and nostalgic journey. The integration with the iPhone 15 Pro and iPhone 15 Pro Max allows users to capture spatial videos on the go and seamlessly relive them on the Apple Vision Pro.

ii. Customizable and Scalable: The App Store Advantage

The App Store on Apple Vision Pro embraces the spatial computing ethos by offering users the ability to arrange and scale apps anywhere in the three-dimensional space. This flexibility ensures that users can tailor their digital environment to suit their preferences, whether it's arranging productivity apps for optimal multitasking or scaling entertainment apps for a more immersive experience.

Developers are encouraged to leverage the unique features of the Apple Vision Pro to create apps that break free from the constraints of traditional displays. This commitment to innovation and creativity is reflected in the diverse array of apps available on the App Store, each offering a distinctive and engaging spatial computing experience.

Conclusion: Navigating the Spatial Horizon

As we conclude our exploration of extraordinary experiences on the Apple Vision Pro, the significance of its role in the spatial computing landscape becomes evident. The device doesn't just offer a new way to interact with digital content; it opens up a three-dimensional frontier where multitasking, collaboration, and familiar apps evolve into a seamless and immersive continuum.

The integration of spatial computing experiences from the new App Store underscores Apple's dedication to fostering innovation within the developer community. Users are not just consumers; they are explorers navigating a spatial horizon filled with possibilities. Whether engaging in productivity tasks, enjoying entertainment, or capturing memories, the Apple Vision Pro transforms each experience into a journey through the spatial realm.

The subsequent chapters will delve deeper into specific aspects of these extraordinary experiences, providing a nuanced understanding of how the Apple Vision Pro becomes an integral part of users' lives. Join us as we unravel the layers of innovation, creativity, and user-centric design that define the Apple Vision Pro's role in shaping the future of spatial computing.

PART 5

The Ultimate Entertainment Experience:

A Cinematic Odyssey with Apple Vision Pro

As we venture into the realm of entertainment, the Apple Vision Pro stands as the harbinger of a new era, promising an unparalleled cinematic odyssey. This chapter delves into the facets that define the Apple Vision Pro as the ultimate entertainment device, exploring its ultra-high-resolution displays and seamless support for content providers, the groundbreaking Apple Immersive Video, and the emergence of new gaming experiences, all navigated through the immersive App Store designed exclusively for the Apple Vision Pro.

A. Ultra-High-Resolution Displays and Support for Content Providers

i. Visual Prowess: The Power of Ultra-High-Resolution

At the heart of the Apple Vision Pro's entertainment prowess lies its ultra-high-resolution displays. Boasting more pixels than a 4K TV for each eye, the device immerses users in a visual feast where clarity and detail redefine the standards of display technology. The ultra-high-resolution displays elevate the viewing experience, transcending traditional boundaries and providing a visual landscape that feels as expansive as it is crisp.

This visual prowess extends beyond conventional displays, offering users a screen that feels 100 feet wide, creating an immersive environment that engulfs the viewer. Whether it's movies, TV shows, or gaming, the ultra-high-resolution displays ensure that every frame is a masterpiece, delivering an entertainment experience that is as breathtaking as it is unprecedented.

ii. Support for Content Providers: A Seamless Streaming Experience

The Apple Vision Pro seamlessly integrates with leading content providers, ensuring users have access to a vast array of entertainment options. Services like Apple TV+, Disney+, and Max harness the capabilities of the ultra-high-resolution displays, delivering content in a visual quality that goes beyond what traditional platforms can offer.

The integration is not limited to streaming services alone; the Apple Vision Pro supports a wide range of content, from movies and TV shows to interactive experiences and spatial videos. This diversity ensures that users can curate their entertainment experience, exploring a world of content that aligns with their preferences and interests.

B. Apple Immersive Video and New Gaming Experiences

i. Apple Immersive Video: A Cinematic Revolution

A pioneering feature introduced by Apple, the Apple Immersive Video format transforms the entertainment landscape. Apple Vision Pro users can delve into a new dimension of storytelling with 180-degree, three-dimensional 8K recordings captured with Spatial Audio. This format places users inside the action, creating an immersive and cinematic experience that blurs the lines between the digital and physical realms.

Imagine being in the front row of a concert, feeling the energy of the crowd, or standing amidst the breathtaking landscapes of a nature documentary. Apple Immersive Video introduces a level of engagement and presence that transcends traditional viewing experiences, making entertainment a truly interactive and participatory endeavor.

ii. New Gaming Experiences: Where Reality Meets the Virtual

Gaming on the Apple Vision Pro transcends traditional boundaries, offering a fusion of reality and the virtual realm. With access to a vast library of games on the App Store, including more than 250 titles on Apple Arcade, users can immerse themselves in gaming experiences that leverage the device's powerful capabilities.

a. Expansive Screen, Immersive Audio: A Gaming Panorama

The ultra-high-resolution displays provide a gaming panorama where visuals are rendered with stunning clarity, and the Spatial Audio enhances the auditory experience, placing users at the center of the gaming universe. Titles like NBA 2K24 Arcade Edition and Sonic Dream Team come to life on a screen as large as users desire, offering an audio-visual spectacle that redefines gaming immersion.

b. Spatial Gaming Experiences: Redefining Play Spaces

The Apple Vision Pro introduces spatial gaming experiences that leverage the device's spatial computing capabilities. Games like Game Room, What the Golf?, and Super Fruit Ninja transform the physical space around players into an integral part of the gaming narrative. Whether it's dodging virtual obstacles in a real-world setting or interacting with spatial elements, these games pioneer a new frontier where reality and virtuality coalesce.

c. Game Controllers and Spatial Control: A Versatile Gaming Interface

Support for popular game controllers ensures that users can choose their preferred method of interaction. The Apple Vision Pro caters to diverse gaming preferences, offering a versatile interface that includes both traditional controls and spatial gestures. This flexibility empowers users to navigate through the gaming landscape in a way that feels most natural to them.

C. App Store for Apple Vision Pro

i. Curated Spatial Experiences: A Showcase of Innovation

The App Store for Apple Vision Pro emerges as a curated marketplace that showcases a myriad of spatial computing experiences. With more than 1 million compatible apps, the App Store becomes a gateway to a world where innovation and creativity flourish. Developers harness the unique capabilities of the Apple Vision Pro, creating apps that redefine entertainment, productivity, and creativity.

a. Productivity Apps in Three Dimensions

Productivity apps like Fantastical and Freeform find new life in the spatial environment, offering users a canvas for brainstorming and collaborating.

The three-dimensional interface transforms the way users engage with these apps, providing an immersive workspace that goes beyond traditional boundaries.

b. Entertainment Experiences Tailored for Vision Pro

Streaming services like Apple TV+, Disney+, and Max offer a catalog of content optimized for ultra-high-resolution displays. Users can access more than 150 3D titles within the Apple TV app, each designed to leverage the immersive capabilities of the Apple Vision Pro. Apple Immersive Video further enriches the entertainment catalog, providing a cinematic experience that goes beyond conventional formats.

c. Gaming Library: A Diverse Array of Experiences

The App Store for Apple Vision Pro boasts a gaming library that caters to a broad spectrum of gaming preferences. From casual gamers to enthusiasts, the curated selection includes titles that leverage the spatial computing capabilities, ensuring that each gaming experience is enhanced by the unique features of the Apple Vision Pro.

ii. Customization and Scalability: Tailoring the Experience

The App Store on Apple Vision Pro goes beyond traditional app marketplaces by offering users the ability to arrange and scale apps anywhere in the three-dimensional space. This customization ensures that users can tailor their digital environment, arranging apps for optimal multitasking or scaling them for a more immersive experience. The spatial computing ethos extends to the App Store, providing users with a dynamic and personalized platform.

Conclusion: Redefining Entertainment, One Frame at a Time

As we navigate the immersive landscape of the Apple Vision Pro's entertainment experience, it becomes evident that the device is not just a viewing platform but a gateway to a new dimension of storytelling, gaming, and interactive content. The ultra-high-resolution displays, support for content providers, Apple Immersive Video, and the App Store curated for spatial experiences collectively redefine entertainment, ushering users into a cinematic odyssey that transcends the boundaries of traditional viewing.

In the subsequent chapters, our journey will continue, exploring specific dimensions of the Apple Vision Pro's impact on entertainment, from the transformative nature of Apple Immersive Video to the spatial gaming experiences that bridge the gap between reality and the virtual realm. Join us as we unravel the layers of innovation, creativity, and user-centric design that define

the Apple Vision Pro's role as the ultimate entertainment device in the spatial computing landscape.

PART VI. Memories Brought to Life: A Journey Through Spatial Time

In the continuum of groundbreaking features that the Apple Vision Pro offers, the chapter on "Memories Brought to Life" stands as a testament to the device's transformative impact on how we capture, relive, and interact with our cherished memories. This exploration delves into the innovative aspects of spatial photos and videos, the enhancements brought about by Spatial Audio, and the seamless integration with the iPhone 15 Pro and iPhone 15 Pro Max, solidifying Apple Vision Pro's role as a custodian of our most treasured moments.

A. Spatial Photos and Videos:

A Quantum Leap in Memory Preservation

i. Time-Traveling Through Images: The Essence of Spatial Photography
The Apple Vision Pro introduces a paradigm shift in the way we capture and relive memories with the introduction of spatial photos. These aren't just static images; they are portals to specific moments in time, imbued with the depth and

dimensionality that traditional photos lack. Each spatial photo becomes a window into the past, allowing users to revisit and immerse themselves in the essence of a particular memory.

Imagine scrolling through a gallery where each photo is more than a snapshot; it's a living, breathing vignette of the moment it encapsulates. The spatial aspect adds a layer of emotional resonance, creating a bridge between the visual and the experiential. Users can traverse through the dimensions of a memory, exploring it from different angles, and feeling the immersive presence of the captured moment.

ii. Cinematic Journeys with Spatial Videos

The concept of spatiality extends beyond photos to videos, ushering in a new era of cinematic storytelling. Spatial videos on the Apple Vision Pro transport users to the heart of the action, offering an immersive journey through recorded moments. The device's ultra-high-resolution displays ensure that each frame is a visual spectacle, while the three-dimensional environment adds a depth that transcends traditional video experiences.

Whether it's a family vacation, a milestone celebration, or a simple day in the park, spatial videos breathe life into the narrative. Users can relive the laughter, feel the warmth, and sense the ambiance as if they were right there in that moment. The marriage of spatial photos and videos elevates memory preservation to an art form, capturing not just the visual details but the emotional nuances that make each memory unique.

B. Spatial Audio Enhancements: Orchestrating Memories with Sound

i. Beyond Visuals: The Impact of Spatial Audio

The Apple Vision Pro recognizes that memories are not solely visual; they are a symphony of sights and sounds. Spatial Audio enhancements ensure that the auditory dimension of memories is as rich and immersive as the visual. As users engage with spatial photos and videos, they are enveloped in a three-dimensional audio experience that complements the spatial visuals.

Imagine watching a spatial video of a live concert. With Spatial Audio, users can feel the music reverberating around them, creating a sense of presence that transcends the boundaries of the device. Each note, each spoken word, becomes an integral part of the memory, enhancing the overall recall and emotional impact.

ii. Seamless Integration: Spatial Audio in Harmony

The integration of Spatial Audio is seamless, making it an intrinsic part of the memory-browsing experience on the Apple Vision Pro. As users navigate through spatial photos and videos, the audio adapts to their perspective, creating a dynamic and responsive auditory environment. This synchronization between visuals and audio ensures that memories are not just seen but felt, fostering a deeper connection with the captured moments.

C. Integration with iPhone 15 Pro and iPhone 15 Pro Max: A Unified Ecosystem

i. Capture and Relive: A Symbiotic Relationship

The Apple Vision Pro doesn't exist in isolation; it is part of a broader ecosystem that seamlessly integrates with the iPhone 15 Pro and iPhone 15 Pro Max. This integration creates a symbiotic relationship where users can capture spatial photos and videos on their iPhones and seamlessly relive them on the Apple Vision Pro.

The process is intuitive and user-friendly. Users can capture spatial videos on the go, ensuring that life's spontaneous moments are preserved in all their three-dimensional glory. Once captured, these spatial memories seamlessly sync with the Apple Vision Pro, where users can explore, relive, and share them in the immersive spatial environment.

ii. Life-Size Scale: From Pocket to Panorama

The integration extends beyond mere compatibility; it offers users the ability to view all their photos and videos at a life-size scale on the Apple Vision Pro. The ultra-high-resolution displays, coupled with the spatial computing capabilities, transform the device into a canvas where memories are not confined to the dimensions of a screen. Panoramas expand and wrap around the user, providing a larger-than-life experience that blurs the lines between the digital and the physical.

Imagine standing amidst towering mountains in a spatial photo or reliving a family gathering at a life-size scale. The integration with the iPhone 15 Pro and iPhone 15 Pro Max allows users to bridge the gap between the everyday and the extraordinary, transforming ordinary moments into extraordinary memories.

Conclusion: A Tapestry of Time and Emotion

As we conclude our exploration of the "Memories Brought to Life" chapter, the Apple Vision Pro emerges not just as a device but as a custodian of the most precious aspects of our lives. The marriage of spatial photos and videos, the orchestration of memories through Spatial Audio, and the seamless integration with the iPhone 15 Pro and iPhone 15 Pro Max weave a tapestry of time and emotion.

In the subsequent chapters, our journey will continue, unraveling the layers of innovation and user-centric design that define the Apple Vision Pro's role in reshaping how we capture, relive, and cherish our memories. Join us as we delve deeper into the extraordinary features that make the Apple Vision Pro not just a technological marvel but a companion on our journey through time and the moments that define us.

PART VII.

FaceTime Becomes Spatial: Redefining Virtual Connectivity

In the ever-evolving landscape of virtual communication, the Apple Vision Pro revolutionizes the way we connect with others through its transformative FaceTime experience. This chapter delves into the groundbreaking features that make FaceTime on the Apple Vision Pro a spatial marvel. From life-size appearances and Spatial Audio that mimics realistic voice locations to the introduction of the Persona feature, we explore how the Apple Vision Pro redefines virtual connectivity, making FaceTime a truly immersive and authentic experience.

A. Life-Size Appearances on FaceTime Calls: Bridging the Virtual Divide

i. Beyond the Screen: The Impact of Life-Size Appearances

FaceTime on the Apple Vision Pro transcends the confines of traditional video calls by introducing life-size appearances. When engaged in a FaceTime call on the Apple Vision Pro, users appear life-size to their counterparts. This transformative feature brings a sense of physical presence to virtual interactions, bridging the gap between the digital and the real.

Imagine conversing with a friend or family member, and instead of a small video window, their life-size representation stands before you. The impact is profound; facial expressions, gestures, and nuances become more pronounced, fostering a sense of connection that goes beyond what standard video calls can achieve. The life-size appearances on FaceTime calls redefine the virtual divide, making virtual interactions more intimate and authentic.

ii. Spatial Context: A Window into Surroundings
The life-size appearances on FaceTime calls also offer a spatial

context by allowing users to see the environment around their counterparts. Whether someone is calling from a bustling city street or a serene countryside, the spatial context enriches the conversation, providing additional layers of connection. This feature goes beyond merely seeing faces; it offers a glimpse into the world that surrounds the person on the other end of the call.

B. Spatial Audio for Realistic Voice Locations: Engaging the Auditory Senses

i. Mimicking Real-World Acoustics

Spatial Audio on FaceTime takes the auditory dimension of virtual communication to new heights. Rather than a monotonous stream of voices, Spatial Audio replicates realistic voice locations. When engaged in a FaceTime call, users perceive the spatial location of the voices, creating a dynamic and immersive auditory experience.

Imagine a group FaceTime call where voices come from different directions, simulating the sensation of being in a physical space with multiple speakers. This not only adds a layer of realism to the conversation but also makes it easier to distinguish between speakers, enhancing the overall clarity and comprehension of the dialogue.

ii. Adaptive Audio: A Dynamic Auditory Environment

The Spatial Audio feature adapts to the spatial context of the call, creating a dynamic auditory environment. As users move within the spatial environment of the Apple Vision Pro, the audio adjusts accordingly, mimicking the way sounds would change in a real-world setting. This adaptive audio feature ensures that the auditory experience aligns with the visual, creating a seamless and naturalistic communication platform.

C. Persona Feature for Authentic Spatial Representation: A Glimpse into the Real You

i. Creating Authentic Avatars: The Essence of Persona

The Apple Vision Pro introduces the Persona feature, a groundbreaking innovation that adds a layer of authenticity to virtual interactions. Persona goes beyond traditional avatars by creating an authentic spatial representation of the user. Using machine learning techniques, the Persona feature generates a spatial representation that reflects the user's facial expressions and hand movements in real time.

Imagine engaging in a FaceTime call, and instead of a static avatar, your virtual representation mirrors your real-time expressions. Whether it's a smile, a nod, or a wave, the Persona feature captures the nuances that make virtual interactions more genuine. The result is a more authentic and immersive representation, allowing users to express themselves in a spatial context.

ii. Third-Party Integration: Extending Persona Beyond FaceTime

The Persona feature extends beyond the FaceTime ecosystem, integrating with third-party videoconferencing apps such as Zoom, Cisco Webex, and Microsoft Teams. This seamless integration ensures that the authentic spatial representation created by Persona becomes a universal element in virtual communication.

Imagine participating in a work meeting where your colleagues see not just a video feed but an authentic spatial representation of your reactions and engagement. The Persona feature brings a new level of presence to virtual interactions, making them more engaging and meaningful.

Conclusion: Redefining the Essence of Virtual Presence

As we conclude our exploration of how FaceTime becomes spatial on the Apple Vision Pro, it becomes evident that these features go beyond mere technological advancements. They redefine the very essence of virtual presence, making virtual interactions more authentic, engaging, and immersive.

In the subsequent chapters, our journey will continue, unraveling the layers of innovation and user-centric design that define the Apple Vision Pro's role in reshaping how we connect with others in the digital realm. Join us as we delve deeper into the extraordinary features that make the Apple Vision Pro not just a technological marvel but a catalyst for redefining the landscape of virtual connectivity.

PART VIII.

Breakthrough Design: Crafting Personalized Spatial Experiences

In the realm of technological innovation, the Apple Vision Pro doesn't merely stand out for its advanced features but also for its breakthrough design that redefines the expectations of wearables. This chapter delves into the meticulous details of the Apple Vision Pro's design, exploring the modular approach for personalization, the fusion of three-dimensionally formed laminated glass and a custom aluminum alloy frame, and the incorporation of ZEISS Optical Inserts for vision correction needs.

A. Modular Design for Personalization: Tailoring the Spatial Experience

i. Unveiling Personalization Possibilities

The Apple Vision Pro breaks away from the one-size-fits-all approach with its innovative modular design. Recognizing the diverse preferences and anatomical variations among users, Apple introduces a system that allows individuals to personalize their fit for optimal comfort and functionality.

At the core of this design philosophy are flexible components that users can adjust according to their preferences. The Light Seal, a crucial element for blocking external light, comes in various shapes and sizes, ensuring a precise fit that conforms to the contours of the user's face. Additionally, the inclusion of both the Solo Knit Band and Dual Loop Band provides users with options to find the perfect balance between stability and comfort.

ii. The Power of Personalized Audio

Audio, a fundamental aspect of the spatial computing experience, is also tailored to individual needs. The flexible straps ensure that the speakers remain in close proximity to the user's ears, optimizing audio delivery. This not only enhances the overall audio quality but also contributes to the immersive nature of spatial experiences, where sound plays a pivotal role in creating a sense of presence.

B. Three-Dimensionally Formed, Laminated Glass, and Custom Aluminum Alloy Frame: Aesthetic Sophistication Meets Durability

i. The Aesthetics of Glass

The visual appeal of the Apple Vision Pro is a testament to the marriage of aesthetics and functionality. The device features a singular piece of three-dimensionally formed, laminated glass that gently curves around the user's face. This design choice serves multiple purposes, offering a sleek and futuristic appearance while maintaining the robustness necessary for a device meant to be worn daily.

The three-dimensionally formed glass is more than a design element; it contributes to the immersive experience by seamlessly integrating the digital content with the physical world. The curvature ensures a snug fit, minimizing light leakage, and enhancing the overall effectiveness of the device.

ii. Custom Aluminum Alloy Frame: Engineering Excellence
Complementing the glass is a custom aluminum alloy frame, a hallmark of Apple's commitment to engineering excellence. This frame provides the necessary structural support,

ensuring durability without compromising on weight. The balance achieved between strength and weight is crucial for a device designed to be worn for extended periods, making the Apple Vision Pro both resilient and comfortable.

The custom aluminum alloy frame not only reinforces the device's structural integrity but also serves as a canvas for the intersection of form and function. The sleek and minimalistic design language echoes Apple's signature style, creating a device that is not just a technological marvel but a fashion statement in the world of wearables.

iii. Light Seal: A Soft Textile Innovation

Nestled within the frame is the Light Seal, a soft textile that plays a pivotal role in ensuring an optimal spatial experience. This component, available in various shapes and sizes, flexes to conform to the unique contours of each user's face, blocking external light and enhancing the immersive nature of the device. The Light Seal goes beyond functionality; it represents a commitment to user comfort and the meticulous attention to detail that defines Apple's design philosophy.

C. ZEISS Optical Inserts for Vision Correction Needs: A Clear Vision of Inclusivity

i. Vision Correction in the Spatial Realm

Recognizing the diverse visual needs of users, Apple collaborates with ZEISS to introduce Optical Inserts for the Apple Vision Pro. These inserts cater to individuals with vision correction requirements, ensuring that the device remains inclusive and accessible to a wide range of users.

The ZEISS Optical Inserts offer two options: readers and prescription inserts. Readers provide a magnified view for users with presbyopia or other mild vision impairments, enhancing the clarity of the display. On the other hand, prescription inserts are customized to individual vision prescriptions, ensuring that users with more specific visual needs can experience the full sharpness and clarity of the Apple Vision Pro's display.

ii. Magnetic Attachment: Seamlessness in Correction

The implementation of ZEISS Optical Inserts is not just about addressing vision correction needs; it's about doing so seamlessly. The inserts magnetically attach to the Apple Vision Pro, aligning precisely with the user's eyes and ensuring that the corrective lenses maintain the optimal distance for visual clarity.

This magnetic attachment mechanism adds a layer of convenience, allowing users to switch between corrected and non-corrected vision effortlessly. Whether someone needs prescription lenses or simply requires reading glasses, the ZEISS Optical Inserts exemplify Apple's commitment to creating a spatial computing device that caters to the diverse needs of its user base.

Conclusion: A Harmonious Fusion of Form and Function

As we conclude our exploration of the breakthrough design of the Apple Vision Pro, it becomes evident that this is more than just a wearable device; it's a harmonious fusion of form and function. The modular approach for personalization, the marriage of three-dimensionally formed laminated glass with a custom aluminum alloy frame, and the inclusivity brought about by ZEISS Optical Inserts collectively redefine the standards for wearable technology.

In the upcoming chapters, our journey will continue, delving into the core technologies and performance capabilities that make the Apple Vision Pro not only a design marvel but a pioneer in reshaping the landscape of spatial computing. Join us as we unravel the layers of innovation that define the very essence of the Apple Vision Pro.

PART X

Unrivaled Innovation: Redefining the Boundaries of Spatial Computing

In the pursuit of pushing the boundaries of spatial computing, the Apple Vision Pro stands as a testament to unrivaled innovation. This chapter delves into the three pillars that form the backbone of the device's groundbreaking capabilities: the ultra-high-resolution display system employing micro-OLED technology, the high-performance eye tracking system, and the revolutionary dual-chip design featuring the M2 and R1 chips.

A. Ultra-High-Resolution Display System Using Micro-OLED Technology: A Visual Spectacle

i. The Technological Marvel of Micro-OLED

At the heart of the Apple Vision Pro's visual prowess lies its ultra-high-resolution display system, powered by micro-OLED technology. This technological marvel takes visual experiences to unprecedented levels by packing 23 million pixels into displays the size of postage stamps. The result is a visual spectacle that redefines the standards for clarity, sharpness, and vibrancy in the realm of spatial computing.

Micro-OLED technology marks a significant leap forward in display innovation. The tiny, individually lit pixels contribute to not only stunning visual fidelity but also more efficient power consumption. The integration of micro-OLED ensures that every detail, every color, and every nuance in the digital content is rendered with unparalleled precision, creating an immersive canvas for spatial experiences.

ii. Beyond 4K: Elevating the Visual Experience

The Apple Vision Pro's ultra-high-resolution displays transcend the capabilities of traditional 4K TVs. Each eye benefits from a display that surpasses the pixel count of a 4K TV, delivering an unrivaled visual feast. This elevated visual experience is not just about pixel count; it's about the convergence of advanced technologies to create a display that feels 100 feet wide, pulling users into a spatial realm that blurs the lines between the digital and the physical.

B. High-Performance Eye Tracking System and the EyeSight Feature: Connecting Through Gazes

i. Responsive Interaction: The Power of Eye Tracking

The high-performance eye tracking system embedded in the Apple Vision Pro represents a paradigm shift in how users interact with spatial computing. High-speed cameras, coupled with a ring of LEDs projecting invisible light patterns onto the user's eyes, enable responsive and intuitive input. The device seamlessly tracks the user's gaze, translating subtle eye movements into meaningful actions within the spatial environment.

The responsive nature of the eye tracking system extends beyond navigation. It becomes a fundamental aspect of how users connect with others through the groundbreaking EyeSight feature. When a person wearing the Apple Vision Pro approaches someone, the device turns transparent, allowing the user to see the other person while simultaneously displaying the user's eyes. This intuitive feature enhances real-world connections, making the device a seamless extension of interpersonal communication.

ii. EyeSight: Visual Cues for Connection

EyeSight goes beyond its transparency feature; it becomes a visual language for communication in the spatial realm. When a user is immersed in an environment or engaged with an app, EyeSight provides visual cues to those around them, indicating the user's focus. This innovative feature transforms the Apple Vision Pro from a personal device to a communicative tool, fostering a deeper connection between users in shared spaces.

C. Dual-Chip Design with M2 and R1 Chips for Powerful Performance: The Brains Behind the Brilliance

i. M2 Chip: Powering Standalone Performance

At the core of the Apple Vision Pro's computing prowess is the M2 chip, a testament to Apple's commitment to delivering powerful and standalone performance. This chip represents the culmination of Apple's expertise in chip design, offering a seamless and responsive experience for users engaging with spatial computing.

The M2 chip not only drives the device's performance but also lays the foundation for the fluidity and responsiveness of the spatial interface. Whether users are navigating immersive environments, interacting with three-dimensional interfaces, or enjoying content with ultra-high resolution, the M2 chip ensures a computing experience that is both powerful and energy-efficient.

ii. R1 Chip: Processing Spatial Input with Precision

In tandem with the M2 chip, the Apple Vision Pro introduces the revolutionary R1 chip, specifically designed to process input from 12 cameras, five sensors, and six microphones. This dual-chip design ensures that spatial input is not only precise but also responsive to the nuances of user interactions.

The R1 chip plays a crucial role in enhancing the overall spatial computing experience. It processes the intricate data streams from multiple sensors, enabling the device to interpret and respond to user inputs with a level of accuracy that defines the Apple Vision Pro's user-centric design. The result is an immersive and intuitive spatial interface that seamlessly integrates with the user's natural movements and gestures.

Conclusion: A Symphony of Technological Innovation

As we conclude our exploration of the unrivaled innovation embedded in the Apple Vision Pro, it becomes clear that this device is more than a wearable—it's a symphony of technological marvels orchestrated to redefine spatial computing. The ultra-high-resolution display system, high-performance eye tracking system, and the dual-chip design collectively contribute to an immersive and intuitive spatial experience.

In the upcoming chapters, our journey will continue, unraveling the layers of functionality and user-centric design that make the Apple Vision Pro a pioneer in reshaping the landscape of spatial computing. Join us as we delve deeper into the extraordinary features that define the very essence of the Apple Vision Pro.

PART XI Privacy and Security: Safeguarding the Spatial Realm

In the ever-evolving landscape of spatial computing, privacy and security are paramount considerations. The Apple Vision Pro takes a pioneering stance in this realm, introducing innovative features and measures to ensure a secure and private spatial computing experience. This chapter explores the three pillars of privacy and security within the Apple Vision Pro: the Optic ID for iris-based authentication, privacy considerations during navigation, and the nuanced privacy aspects of the EyeSight visual cues for others.

A. Optic ID for Iris-Based Authentication: A Gaze into Secure Access

i. Iris Authentication: Elevating Security Measures

At the forefront of privacy and security in the Apple Vision Pro is the Optic ID, an iris-based authentication system. Leveraging the distinct patterns of the user's iris, Optic ID serves as a secure and personalized means of unlocking the device, autofilling passwords, and completing payments with Apple Pay.

Iris authentication represents a sophisticated layer of security, surpassing traditional methods such as passwords or facial recognition. The uniqueness and complexity of the iris patterns provide a secure biometric identifier, significantly reducing the risk of unauthorized access. Optic ID ensures that access to the spatial computing realm of the Apple Vision Pro is exclusive to the rightful owner, adding a robust layer of protection to sensitive data and personal content.

ii. Seamless Integration: A User-Friendly Approach

While Optic ID prioritizes security, it does so without compromising user convenience. The seamless integration of iris authentication ensures that unlocking the Apple Vision Pro is a swift and intuitive process. Users can effortlessly access their personalized spatial environment with a simple gaze, eliminating the need for cumbersome passwords or intricate authentication procedures.

This user-friendly approach to security aligns with Apple's commitment to creating technology that is both secure and accessible. Optic ID exemplifies how advanced security measures can coexist with a seamless and intuitive user experience, making privacy a natural extension of the user's interaction with the device.

B. Privacy Considerations During Navigation: Navigating the Spatial Realm Safely

i. Where You Look Stays Private: Navigating Without Intrusion

Privacy is not just about securing access to the device; it's also about ensuring that users can navigate the spatial realm without unnecessary intrusion. The Apple Vision Pro prioritizes user privacy by ensuring that where users look stays private during navigation.

As users explore immersive environments, interact with three-dimensional interfaces, or engage with spatial applications, the Apple Vision Pro maintains a discreet approach to tracking gaze. The device refrains from sharing the user's gaze information with external entities, including Apple itself. This commitment to privacy during navigation extends to the core of the spatial computing experience, allowing users to explore and interact with confidence in the security of their personal space.

ii. Gaze Data Confidentiality: A Fundamental Principle

The gaze data captured by the Apple Vision Pro is treated with the utmost confidentiality. Apple ensures that gaze information is not shared with third-party apps, websites, or any external entities. This commitment to data privacy extends beyond the device itself, reflecting Apple's dedication to safeguarding user information throughout the spatial computing ecosystem.

By maintaining the confidentiality of gaze data, the Apple Vision Pro sets a precedent for responsible and privacy-centric spatial computing. Users can navigate, interact, and engage with content, knowing that their gaze remains a private aspect of their personal experience.

C. EyeSight Visual Cues for Others: Transparency in Spatial Interaction

i. Visual Cues for Spatial Transparency

The EyeSight feature, a groundbreaking aspect of the Apple Vision Pro, introduces visual cues for others in shared spaces. While this feature enhances communication and connection, it also raises considerations for the privacy of the user's interactions. Apple addresses these concerns by ensuring that the EyeSight visual cues strike a delicate balance between transparency and privacy.

When a user is engaged in an environment or an app, EyeSight provides visual cues to those around them, indicating the user's focus or interaction points. However, Apple ensures that this information is presented in a way that respects the user's privacy. The cues are designed to be informative without being intrusive, allowing for spatial transparency without compromising the confidentiality of the user's spatial computing activities.

ii. Managing Privacy Preferences: User Control Over Visual Cues

Recognizing the diversity of user preferences, the Apple Vision Pro empowers users with control over their privacy settings. Users can manage and customize the visual cues generated by EyeSight, tailoring the level of transparency and information shared with others. This level of user control reflects Apple's commitment to providing a personalized and secure spatial computing experience.

By allowing users to define their privacy preferences, Apple ensures that the EyeSight feature enhances spatial transparency while respecting individual boundaries. This approach aligns with Apple's user-centric design philosophy, where privacy is not just a default setting but a customizable aspect of the user experience.

Conclusion: Elevating Privacy and Security in Spatial Computing

As we conclude our exploration of privacy and security within the Apple Vision Pro, it becomes evident that these considerations are not mere add-ons but integral components of the device's design philosophy. The Optic ID for iris-based authentication, privacy considerations during navigation, and the nuanced approach to EyeSight visual cues collectively contribute to an elevated standard of privacy and security in the spatial computing realm.

In the upcoming chapters, our journey will continue, delving into the immersive experiences and practical applications that define the Apple Vision Pro as a trailblazer in the world of spatial computing. Join us as we uncover the layers of innovation that make this device not only groundbreaking in technology but also exemplary in prioritizing user privacy and security.

PART XII Accessibility in visionOS: Empowering Inclusivity and User Freedom

In the realm of spatial computing, accessibility is a cornerstone that determines the inclusivity of a device. The Apple Vision Pro, with its visionOS, is designed to be a beacon of inclusivity, ensuring that users of all abilities can engage with the spatial computing experience seamlessly. This chapter delves into the two fundamental aspects of accessibility within visionOS: the integration of key accessibility features and the support for multiple input methods.

A. Integration of Key Accessibility Features: Paving the Way for Inclusive Interaction

i. VoiceOver: A Guiding Voice in the Spatial Realm

VoiceOver, a longstanding accessibility feature in Apple's ecosystem, takes on new dimensions within the spatial computing landscape of the Apple Vision Pro. This screen reader, known for its

ii. Zoom: Amplifying the Spatial Experience

Zoom, another key accessibility feature, plays a crucial role in enhancing the spatial experience for users with visual challenges. In the spatial computing context, Zoom goes beyond traditional screen magnification. It allows users to focus on specific elements within the spatial environment, providing a closer look at digital content and enhancing the overall visibility of details.

The dynamic nature of spatial computing, with its immersive environments and three-dimensional interfaces, necessitates adaptive accessibility features. Zoom, tailored for the spatial realm, exemplifies Apple's commitment to providing users with diverse abilities the tools they need to engage meaningfully with the Apple Vision Pro.

iii. Switch Control: Navigating Spatial Interfaces with Precision

Switch Control, an accessibility feature that enables users with motor impairments to interact with devices using external switches, takes on new significance within the context of visionOS. The three-dimensional user interface, controlled by a user's eyes, hands, and voice, is complemented by

Switch Control, offering an additional method for precise navigation.

Users can seamlessly transition between spatial environments, select apps, and interact with elements using external switches. The integration of Switch Control underscores Apple's dedication to ensuring that the spatial computing experience is accessible to users with diverse motor abilities, empowering them to navigate the digital realm with precision.

B. Support for Multiple Input Methods: Tailoring Interaction to Individual Preferences

i. Pointer Control: Choosing the Preferred Input Method

visionOS on the Apple Vision Pro recognizes that users have diverse preferences when it comes to interacting with spatial interfaces. The introduction of Pointer Control allows users to select their preferred input method, whether it be their eyes, fingers, or wrist.

This flexibility in input methods empowers users to tailor their interaction with the Apple Vision Pro based on their individual preferences and abilities. Whether users find using their eyes most intuitive, prefer the precision of finger gestures, or opt for wrist movements, visionOS adapts to provide a personalized and accessible spatial computing experience.

ii. Dwell Control: Enhancing Interaction Through Pause

Dwell Control is a thoughtful addition to visionOS, designed to enhance the interaction experience for users who may require additional time for precise actions. This feature allows users to pause on an element of visionOS for a few seconds, simulating a tap.

Dwell Control transforms spatial interaction into a more deliberate and controlled process. Users can navigate the three-dimensional interface at their own pace, enjoying the immersive environments and interacting with apps without the constraints of rapid gestures. This feature caters to users with varying motor abilities, ensuring that the spatial computing experience remains adaptable and accommodating.

iii. Voice Control: A Hands-Free Approach to Spatial Interaction
Recognizing the diversity of user preferences and abilities, visionOS incorporates Voice Control as a

primary input method. Users can navigate, interact, and control the Apple Vision Pro entirely through voice commands. This hands-free approach is not only convenient but also ensures that individuals with motor challenges have a reliable and intuitive means of engaging with the spatial computing environment.

Voice Control extends beyond basic commands, allowing users to perform a wide range of activities across the Apple Vision Pro. From opening and closing apps to dictating text and executing spatial gestures, Voice Control serves as a versatile input ability to provide audible descriptions of on-screen elements, is reimagined for the three-dimensional interface of visionOS.

Users with visual impairments can navigate the spatial environment using VoiceOver, receiving auditory cues that describe the spatial layout, the positioning of apps, and interactive elements. The integration of VoiceOver transforms the Apple Vision Pro into a device where individuals with visual impairments can explore and interact with the digital and physical worlds seamlessly.

method, enriching the accessibility of the spatial computing experience.

Conclusion: Shaping a Spatial Landscape of Inclusivity

As we conclude our exploration of accessibility within visionOS, it becomes clear that the Apple Vision Pro is not just a device; it's a gateway to a spatial landscape of inclusivity. The integration of key accessibility features and support for multiple input methods ensure that users of diverse abilities can navigate, explore, and interact with the spatial computing environment on their terms.

In the chapters ahead, our journey will continue, unraveling the layers of innovation that define the Apple Vision Pro as a trailblazer in accessibility and spatial computing. Join us as we delve into the extraordinary features that exemplify the device's commitment to inclusivity and user freedom.

PART XII.

Environmental Considerations: A Sustainable Vision for the Future

In the pursuit of technological innovation, Apple places a strong emphasis on environmental responsibility. The Apple Vision Pro exemplifies this commitment by integrating eco-friendly practices into its design and production. This chapter explores the environmental considerations embedded in the device, focusing on the use of recycled materials, an energy-efficient design, and Apple Vision Pro's adherence to high environmental standards.

A. Use of Recycled Materials and Energy-Efficient Design:
Sustaining Resources, Reducing Impact

i. Recycled Rare Earth Elements: A Commitment to Sustainability
The Apple Vision Pro stands as a testament to Apple's dedication to sustainability, with the inclusion of 100% recycled rare earth elements in all magnets. By incorporating recycled materials into critical components, Apple reduces its

reliance on newly mined resources, minimizing the environmental impact associated with traditional manufacturing processes.

Rare earth elements are crucial for the production of magnets in electronic devices. Apple's decision to utilize recycled rare earth elements in the Apple Vision Pro contributes to the conservation of these valuable resources while simultaneously mitigating the ecological footprint of the device.

ii. Recycled Aluminum Frame and Battery Enclosure: Redefining Device Composition

Furthering its commitment to sustainable practices, the Apple Vision Pro incorporates a frame and battery enclosure made entirely of 100% recycled aluminum. This marks a significant shift in device composition, emphasizing the feasibility and desirability of recycled materials in high-performance electronics.

By opting for recycled aluminum, Apple not only reduces the demand for primary aluminum production but also minimizes energy consumption associated with the extraction and refinement of new aluminum. This strategic choice aligns with Apple's broader goal of creating products that are not only cutting-edge but also environmentally responsible.

iii. Light Seal and Solo Knit Band: A Focus on Recycled Textiles

The commitment to sustainability extends to the exterior components of the Apple Vision Pro, with the Light Seal and Solo Knit Band both constructed using over 70% recycled yarn. These textile components contribute to a significant reduction in the device's overall carbon footprint, promoting a circular economy by repurposing materials.

The use of recycled textiles not only aligns with Apple's environmental goals but also sets a precedent for the industry, showcasing the feasibility of integrating recycled materials into wearable technology without compromising performance or aesthetics.

B. Apple Vision Pro's Adherence to High Environmental Standards:
Setting the Benchmark for Responsible Manufacturing

i. Mercury-Free, Brominated Flame Retardant-Free, PVC-Free, and

Beryllium-Free: Eliminating Hazardous Materials

In line with Apple's stringent environmental standards, the Apple Vision Pro is free of hazardous materials, including mercury, brominated flame retardants, PVC, and beryllium. This commitment to eliminating toxic substances from the device not only ensures user safety but also reduces the environmental impact associated with the disposal of electronic waste.

By adhering to these high environmental standards, Apple not only prioritizes the well-being of its users but also actively contributes to the reduction of electronic waste pollution, aligning with global efforts to create a more sustainable and circular economy.

ii. Fiber-Based Packaging: A Step Towards Plastic-Free Packaging

Apple's environmental considerations extend to the packaging of the Apple Vision Pro, which is crafted from 100% fiber-based materials. This initiative is a crucial step towards reducing the use of plastics in product packaging, aligning with Apple's ambitious goal of eliminating plastics from all its packaging by 2025.

The shift towards fiber-based packaging reflects a holistic approach to sustainability, addressing not only the device's environmental impact during use but also its entire life cycle, from production to disposal.

Conclusion: Pioneering Sustainability in Spatial Computing

The Apple Vision Pro is not just a technological marvel; it is a beacon of sustainable innovation in the realm of spatial computing. Through the use of recycled materials, an energy-efficient design, and adherence to high environmental standards, Apple sets a benchmark for responsible manufacturing in the tech industry.

As we move forward in our exploration of the Apple Vision Pro, the next chapters will delve into the practical applications and user experiences that define this groundbreaking device. Join us on this journey to uncover the layers of innovation that make the Apple Vision Pro a trailblazer not only in technology but also in sustainability within the spatial computing landscape.

PART XIII.

Pricing and Availability: Navigating the Spatial Frontier

In the ever-evolving landscape of technology, the intersection of innovation and accessibility is often marked by the price and availability of cutting-edge devices. The Apple Vision Pro, with its revolutionary spatial computing capabilities, introduces a new frontier in consumer electronics. This chapter explores the pricing details, storage options, pre-order information, availability dates, and the array of additional accessories available for users to tailor their spatial computing experience.

A. Pricing Details and Storage Options: Crafting the Spatial Experience for Every User

i. Base Pricing and Storage Configurations

The Apple Vision Pro, a pinnacle of spatial computing, is positioned as a device that redefines the boundaries of personal electronics. With a starting price of $3,499 (U.S.), Apple ensures that the transformative power of spatial computing is within reach for enthusiasts and professionals alike. This base pricing includes a generous storage capacity of 256GB, providing users with ample space to store spatial photos, videos, apps, and more.

The pricing strategy reflects Apple's commitment to offering a premium spatial computing experience while maintaining accessibility for a broad user base. The 256GB storage configuration sets a solid foundation for users to immerse themselves in the expansive world of spatial computing without concerns about storage limitations.

ii. Storage Options for Diverse Needs

Recognizing the diverse needs of users, Apple offers the Apple Vision Pro with various storage options to cater to different preferences and usage patterns. Users can choose storage configurations that align with their spatial computing requirements, with options likely extending beyond the base 256GB offering.

The availability of multiple storage options ensures that users can tailor their purchase based on factors such as content creation, gaming, or professional applications, providing a customizable experience that aligns with individual preferences and workflows.

B. Pre-order Information and Availability Dates: Securing a Gateway to the Spatial Realm

i. Commencement of Pre-orders
Anticipation builds as users eagerly await their entry into the spatial realm. Pre-orders for the Apple Vision Pro are set to commence on Friday, January 19, at 5 a.m. PST. This early pre-order date allows enthusiasts and early adopters to secure their devices promptly, ensuring they are among the first to

experience the transformative capabilities of the Apple Vision Pro.

The pre-order phase marks a pivotal moment in the device's journey from announcement to the hands of consumers. Apple enthusiasts and those intrigued by the promise of spatial computing can make their reservations, heralding the imminent arrival of a new era in personal electronics.

ii. Availability Beginning February 2

The spatial frontier officially opens to consumers as the Apple Vision Pro becomes available on Friday,

February 2. On this day, all U.S. Apple Store locations and the U.S. Apple Store online will be stocked with the device, ready to meet the demand generated during the pre-order phase.

The availability date symbolizes the culmination of meticulous engineering, design, and manufacturing efforts, as the Apple Vision Pro makes its way into the hands of users across the United States. This marks a significant milestone in the evolution of spatial computing, with Apple setting the stage for a new era in consumer electronics.

C. Additional Accessories and Their Pricing: Enhancing and Personalizing the Spatial Experience

i. Solo Knit Band and Dual Loop Band

The Apple Vision Pro comes bundled with accessories designed to enhance comfort and personalization. The Solo Knit Band and Dual Loop Band are included with the device, offering users two options for achieving the optimal fit. These bands, crafted with user comfort in mind, ensure that the Apple Vision Pro seamlessly integrates into various lifestyles and preferences.

While the Solo Knit Band and Dual Loop Band are integral components of the Apple Vision Pro package, users can also appreciate the option to purchase additional bands separately. Apple provides a range of band options, allowing users to express their style and further customize the device to suit their personal aesthetic.

ii. ZEISS Optical Inserts — Readers and Prescription

For users with vision correction needs, Apple offers ZEISS Optical Inserts as an accessory, priced at $99 (U.S.) for readers and $149 (U.S.) for prescription inserts. These inserts, designed in collaboration with ZEISS, seamlessly integrate with the Apple Vision Pro, allowing users to experience the device with optimal clarity and sharpness.

The availability of ZEISS Optical Inserts underscores Apple's commitment to inclusivity, ensuring that users with varying vision requirements can fully enjoy the spatial computing experience without compromise. This accessory option adds a layer of personalization to the Apple Vision Pro, addressing the diverse visual needs of its user base.

iii. Apple Vision Pro Cover, Polishing Cloth, and Other Accessories

Complementing the essential components of the Apple Vision Pro, users will find additional accessories within the package. The Apple Vision Pro Cover protects the front of the device, ensuring its pristine condition when not in use. A Polishing Cloth is included for users to maintain the clarity of the advanced display, emphasizing the device's premium nature.

Apple's meticulous attention to detail extends to the accessories, ensuring that users receive a comprehensive package that enhances the overall ownership experience. These accessories, while practical, also contribute to the device's aesthetic appeal, creating a holistic and premium spatial computing package.

Conclusion:
Paving the Way to a Spatial Future
In conclusion, the pricing and availability details of the Apple Vision Pro outline not just a product release but the dawn of a spatial future. The carefully structured pricing, diverse storage options, pre-order commencement, and availability date set the stage for users to embark on a

transformative journey into the spatial realm.

As users explore the limitless possibilities of spatial computing with the Apple Vision Pro, the next chapters will delve into real-world applications, user experiences, and the device's impact on how individuals connect, create, and explore in this new era of personal electronics. Join us as we navigate the spatial frontier together.

Conclusion

Navigating the Spatial Frontier with Apple Vision Pro

As we conclude our exploration of the Apple Vision Pro, a device that transcends the boundaries of conventional personal electronics, we reflect on the key points that define its significance in the landscape of spatial computing. From its groundbreaking features to its commitment to accessibility and sustainability, the Apple Vision Pro stands as a harbinger of a new era in consumer electronics.

A. Summary of Key Points

The journey through the chapters of this exploration has unveiled the intricate layers of innovation woven into the fabric of the Apple Vision Pro:

1. Revolutionary Spatial Computing: The Apple Vision Pro introduces a paradigm shift with its spatial computing capabilities, seamlessly blending the digital and physical worlds through its visionOS and three-dimensional user interface.

2. Inclusivity Through Accessibility: The device exemplifies Apple's commitment to inclusivity, integrating key accessibility features like VoiceOver, Zoom, Switch Control, and more. Users can engage with the spatial realm using their

eyes, hands, voice, or a combination tailored to their preferences.

3. Unparalleled Entertainment Experiences: Boasting ultra-high-resolution displays, support for content providers, and the innovative Apple Immersive Video, the Apple Vision Pro delivers an immersive entertainment experience that transcends traditional boundaries.

4. Memories Brought to Life: Spatial photos, videos, and Spatial Audio transport users to cherished moments, offering a unique and immersive way to relive memories.

Integration with the iPhone 15 Pro and iPhone 15 Pro Max enhances the versatility of capturing and experiencing spatial content.

5. Spatial FaceTime and Persona: The spatial representation of FaceTime calls, coupled with the creation of a Persona, transforms virtual interactions. Users appear life-size, and the spatial audio enhances the realism of communication.

6. Breakthrough Design: The modular design, three-dimensionally formed laminated glass, custom aluminum alloy frame, and adaptable

bands showcase Apple's prowess in design and user personalization.

7. Unrivaled Innovation: The Apple Vision Pro's ultra-high-resolution display system, high-performance eye tracking, and the unique dual-chip design with M2 and R1 chips demonstrate Apple's commitment to pushing the boundaries of what is technologically possible.

8. Privacy and Security: The Optic ID for iris-based authentication, privacy considerations during navigation, and the innovative EyeSight feature

contribute to making the Apple Vision Pro a secure and privacy-focused device.

9. Accessibility in visionOS: The integration of VoiceOver, Zoom, Switch Control, and support for multiple input methods ensures that the spatial computing experience is accessible to users with diverse abilities.

10. Environmental Considerations: The use of recycled materials, an energy-efficient design, and adherence to high environmental standards underscore Apple's commitment to sustainability.

11. Pricing and Availability: With a carefully structured pricing strategy, diverse storage options, and a comprehensive set of accessories, Apple ensures that the Apple Vision Pro is both accessible and customizable to a broad user base.

B. The Potential Impact on the VR Industry

The introduction of the Apple Vision Pro heralds a potential transformation in the Virtual Reality (VR) industry. By seamlessly integrating spatial computing into a consumer device, Apple has democratized access to immersive experiences. The device's focus on accessibility, innovative features, and ecosystem integration positions it as a catalyst for mainstream adoption of spatial computing.

The impact is not confined to the user experience alone; Apple's entry into the VR space is likely to spur advancements in content creation, application development, and the overall evolution of the VR ecosystem. Developers now have a platform with the potential to reach millions, driving innovation and pushing the boundaries of what is achievable in the spatial computing landscape.

C. Closing Thoughts on the Future of Spatial Computing

As we stand on the precipice of a spatial computing revolution, the Apple Vision Pro beckons us to reimagine how we connect, create, and explore. It represents more than just a device; it signifies the advent of a new era where the digital and physical worlds harmonize seamlessly.

The future of spatial computing is inherently tied to the evolution of technology and its integration into our daily lives. The Apple Vision Pro paves the way for a future where spatial interactions become as natural as the physical world, where the boundaries between reality and the digital realm blur, and where innovation in personal electronics is synonymous with a commitment to accessibility and sustainability.

In the chapters yet to be written in the spatial computing narrative, the Apple Vision Pro stands as a beacon, guiding us towards a future where the extraordinary becomes ordinary, and where the spatial frontier is not just navigated but embraced as an integral part of our connected existence. As users embark on their journeys with the Apple Vision Pro, they step into a spatial realm that is not just about technology; it's about the limitless possibilities that unfold when imagination and innovation converge. The spatial future awaits, and the Apple Vision Pro is at the forefront, shaping the way forward.

USER GUIDE WILL BE RELEASED AS SOON AS THE PRODUCT IS RELEASED ON JANUARY 19.

www.ingramcontent.com/pod-product-compliance
Lightning Source LLC
LaVergne TN
LVHW051330050326
832903LV00031B/3464